Monsters
Myth or Fact?

Thea
Feldman

P9-CQJ-269

SCHOLASTIC INC.
New York Toronto London Auckland
Sydney Mexico City New Delhi Hong Kong

Read more! Do more!

After you read this book, download your free all-new digital activities.

You can show what a great reader you are!

Monsters
reading fun
enter

For Mac and PC

Monster hotel
Which monsters are lurking behind the doors of this horrible hotel?
Click on the correct answer, then watch what jumps out!

Take quizzes about the fun facts in this book!

Make a flying dragon
Would you like to create your own monster? Follow the steps to make this fiery dragon that can flap its wings. Why not hang it in your bedroom?

Now click the numbers . . .

1 2 3 4 5 6

You will need . . .
Sticky tape
White card
Crayons or markers
Thread
Scissors
Red and orange tissue paper for flames
Glue stick

Do fun activities with simple step-by-step instructions!

Log on to

www.scholastic.com/discovermore/readers

Enter this special code: **L2HJC6HCG2P2**

2

Contents

ISBN 978-0-545-83946-4

12 11 10 9 8 7 6 5 4 3   15 16 17 18 19 20/0

Printed in the U.S.A.   40
This edition first printing, September 2015

Myth or fact?

Look out! A 50-foot giant lifts up its head and roars. It's a monster! Or is it? Maybe it's a giant lizard or another terrifying animal.

Long ago, explorers traveled to far-off places. They told tales of the monsters they saw on their travels. Their children told the stories to their children. In time, the stories became myths.

5

Are the monsters of myth real? Or do our imaginations play tricks on us? Are mythical monsters actually things from the natural world? Do you dare meet some . . . and find out?

Dragon
(page 8)

Ogopogo
(page 12)

Loch Ness Monster
(page 13)

Leviathan
(page 16)

Kraken
(page 18)

Yeti
(page 20)

Vampire
(page 24)

Bigfoot
(page 22)

Dragons

Some fly. Some slither. Some breathe fire. Some bring good luck. Some are evil. All are dragons!

Myths about dragons come from all over the world. In Europe, beware! The dragon is a winged, fire-breathing creature, ready to do battle with its enemies. In China, celebrate! The dragon means life and good fortune.

DRAGONS AROUND THE WORLD

Japanese

Indian

European

Chinese

Many real-life animals are named for dragons. The creature most like a mythical dragon is the Komodo dragon. It is the world's largest lizard.

It's a fact!

Komodo dragon

The largest Komodo dragon was more

It lives in the jungle in Indonesia. It does not breathe fire, but it has a deadly bite. Its bite is poisonous and kills within 24 hours.

It roars! The frilled lizard puffs out its frill to scare other animals.

It flies! The flying dragon is a little lizard. It glides from tree to tree.

than 10 feet long and weighed 366 pounds.

Lake monsters

Okanagan Lake in Canada looks calm and quiet. But watch out! Many people say that they have seen a 50-foot monster, shaped like a huge snake, rise from the water. The monster is called Ogopogo.

Okanagan Lake

Loch Ness

In Scotland, hundreds of people say that they have seen a monster with a very long neck and tail swimming in Loch Ness. They call it the Loch Ness Monster, or Nessie.

Surprise! Ogopogo rises above the water's surface. Could this monster be hiding in the deep lake?

Could Ogopogo and Nessie be real? People watch for them, and they take photos and videos. But our eyes can play tricks on us.

It's a fact!

People have been talking

Is that a monster? Is it a big log in the water? Is it a real animal? Or is it something else?

Can you see Ogopogo? No. The big log looks like a monster.

Is this Nessie? No. It is a gray seal, just 10 feet long.

Is this Nessie? No. This photo, taken in 1934, turned out to be a fake.

about the Loch Ness Monster since 565 CE!

Monsters of the sea

Since ancient times, sailors have told myths about sea monsters. One was about a giant sea animal with smoke coming out of its nose. This monster, Leviathan, was so strong that neither arrows nor swords could kill it.

Today, people think that Leviathan was some sort of whale. Whales do not attack people, but they really are giants! The blue whale is the world's biggest real animal. It can be more than 100 feet long.

BIGGEST SEA CREATURES

Blue whale (108 feet)

Sperm whale (79 feet)

Whale shark (62 feet)

Basking shark (40 feet)

Giant squid (40 feet)

A lone ship sails on the sea. All of a sudden, the Kraken rises up! The huge monster surrounds the ship with its long arms. The sailors on board shout in terror. They try to fight back. But the Kraken pulls the ship full of people down under the water.

The giant squid lives in the very deepest parts of the ocean. It looks like the Kraken.

Giant, hairy monsters

People talk about a tall, hairy monster stomping around in the mountains. They call it the Yeti, or the Abominable Snowman. It is said to live in the Himalayas in Asia.

Monster footprints?
Footprints 17 inches long have been found in the snow.

Bear   **Human**   **Yeti?**

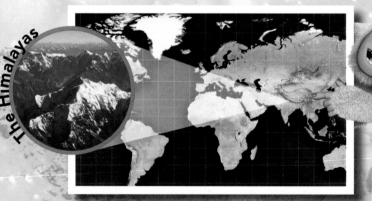

The Himalayas

Dozens of explorers have tried to find it, or some proof that it exists. All of them have failed.

NEW WORD

abominable
uh-BAH-muh-nuh-buhl
Things that are truly horrible are **abominable**.

SAY IT OUT LOUD

21

People have seen
a big, hairy giant in
North America, too.
Bigfoot, also called
Sasquatch, is at
least 6 and a half
feet tall. It weighs
more than 500
pounds and
has footprints
2 feet long!

Bigfoot and the Yeti look a lot like gorillas. Could they be a new kind of ape? But where they live is too cold for apes. Are they just bears standing on their hind legs?

Jane Goodall is a chimpanzee expert. She says about Bigfoot: "Why isn't there a body? . . . Maybe they don't exist, but I want them to."

Vampires

Be extra careful after the sun goes down. Why? Because, many myths say, that's when vampires attack. They bite people on their necks and suck their blood! And if a vampire bites you, you become one, too! The best-known vampire is Dracula. He isn't real, but he is based on a real-life prince.

It's a fact!

The real prince Dracula lived in the

1400s. He was cruel and bloodthirsty.

Vampires are not real. But there are real animals that suck blood! The vampire bat is one. It sucks blood from animals but does not hurt them. A mother vampire bat can suck blood, then throw it up to feed her babies!

Bats are the only mammals that can fly.

Bats fold their wings and hang upside down to sleep.

Bats hunt at night, using sound. They have sharp hearing.

A vampire bat makes a tiny bite with its teeth, then licks an animal's blood.

More monsters

People love to scare themselves with stories about monsters! Here are a few more!

A-woo!

Werewolf

A werewolf is a man who changes into a wolf when there is a full moon. Is it really just a big, scary wolf?

Ogre

An ogre is a large monster that eats people. It's not real!

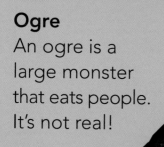

Unicorn

Long ago, people thought the tusks of a sea animal, the narwhal, were unicorn horns.

Narwhal

Troll

A troll is an ugly beast that lives in a cave with other trolls and bothers people.

Mermaid

Some myths say mermaids bring terrible storms. Others say they bring good luck. When sailors saw mermaids, were they really seeing manatees?

Manatee

Zombie

A dead person who comes back to life and eats living people is a zombie.

Boo!

Glossary

abominable
Disgusting or horrible.

ape
A hairy mammal that is related to monkeys.

bloodthirsty
Eager for or enjoying violence.

chimpanzee
A small ape that has dark hair and lives in Africa.

exist
To be real.

explorer
A person who travels in order to discover new places and things.

fact
A piece of information that is known to be true.

fail
To be unable to do something.

glide
To move through the air smoothly and easily.

gorilla
A large ape that has dark hair and wide shoulders and lives in Africa.

lizard
An animal with a scaly body, four legs, and a long tail.

lone
Alone.

mammal
An animal that has hair or fur, breathes air, and makes milk to feed its young.

manatee
A large, plant-eating mammal with flippers and a flat tail. Manatees live in warm waters near coasts.

myth
An old story that describes the beliefs or history of a group of people. Some myths were created to explain things in nature that people couldn't understand.

mythical
Imaginary or untrue; having to do with myths.

narwhal
A large mammal that lives in cold waters. A male narwhal has one long, twisted tusk.

natural world
The world of nature, including air, land, water, plants, and animals.

poisonous
Capable of causing sickness or death.

proof
Information that shows that something is true.

roar
To make a loud, long, deep sound.

slither
To move along by sliding, like a snake.

squid
A sea animal with a long, soft body and ten arms.

tusk
A long, pointed tooth that sticks out of the mouth.

Index